THE POISON PRISON

INSIDE THE MIND OF A PARANOID SCHIZOPHRENIC

POETRY BY

CHRIS MAOATE

Revised Edition

ISBN Kindle: 978-0-473-47052-4
ISBN Epub: 978-0-473-4705214
ISBN On Demand Print: 978-0-473-48485-9

**This book is for all those people who
never belonged...**

...welcome home.

About the Author

I've been diagnosed with Paranoid Schizophrenia for over 25 years. My story is a common one. Overdoses, self harm, isolation, chain smoking, obesity, depression, obsessive compulsive disorder, panic attacks, inability to work full time, inability to maintain friendships (except one), fear of intimate relationships, fear I'll always be alone.

Writing helps me to understand myself better. Sometimes after I write I think to myself " Oh that's why I'm like that." Each poem unlocks a gate which then takes me deeper and closer to the core.

When I first began writing this book over twenty years ago it was my intention to attack the mental health system. It wasn't until its completion that I realized I wasn't angry at them. Throughout the writing process I thought I was meant to be the teacher. It wasn't until I finished the book that I realized I had become it's student.

Trigger Warning

This book contains some strong themes around domestic violence. Please stop reading this book if it causes an emotional disturbance or has any other adverse effects on you.

Table of Contents

PART ONE

Treason is the Brother of Authenticity

The Dark Knight

Who knew that being a villain could be so cool. In my opinion it's only Christopher Nolan that could achieve this. Both Heath Ledger and Tom Hardy's characters outshone our superhero.

But why...?

Make no mistake Bale as Batman was a much darker version of the bat that we had not seen before, (except briefly with Mike Keaton.)

I think darkness intrigues all of us. The clean-cut superhero of old has outworn its costume. No one really associates to the angelic no-fault 'I can do no wrong' characters because they don't exist.

We relate to heroes with faults, flaws, and serious defects because we need this. Sinister, dark and even mad superheroes reflect back to us our own path to redemption.

Maybe that's the makeup of a true superhero. One that neither fears death, darkness nor madness but embraces them.

2 Hold Back God's Wrath

Ten good men would have stopped
The destruction of Sodom and Gomorrah
Cancelled God's wrath
Withheld their slaughter
That was God's promise
To hold back the tide
All I needed was just one
In this journey of life

A protector and shelter
From the worst of the weather
Someone not afraid to ponder
Something much heavier

One reliable soul
To give me sanctuary to hide
Someone to pull me out
When I retreat too deep inside

One brave soldier
To stand in my line of fire
Who'll never submit nor surrender
If the battle rages higher

One true friend
Who'll never throw in the towel
Nor walk away
When they poison the well

All I needed was just one
To hold back the tide
To save me from the chaos
And destruction inside

I needed one righteous man
To hold back the wrath
Who could have shone a light
To help me find the way back
But just like Lot's wife
That part died long ago
Each time I think back
My legs return to pillars of salt

Jester

The Jester will make you laugh
He will take you from lows to highs
He'll play games all for fun
But it's hard to know what's inside
He's got masks he wears for your benefit
Costumes with bells on too
He's got a costume that won't let you know
What troubles he's been through
He'll tale a thousand different tales
Play a thousand different tunes
He'll do cartwheels from wall to wall
Just to ease your blues
But the Jester can't play forever
Sooner or later he faces a time
When the laughter from the crowd stops
And he has to face his own sigh

My Father's Son

I'll learn to toil this soil by hand
I'll drink until I'm done
I'll run from those things I cannot face
I am my fathers son

We are so, so different
Yet just the same
Filled with burning ambition
Yet ordinary and plain

I'll make education my religion
Put my faith in God
Strip away all their uniqueness
I shall not spare the rod

I'll invite the darkness in
Rule this kingdom with fear
I'll hit you harder still
If you can't hold back the tears

He use to stitch his lips together
Except when he had his fill
I bury myself in silence
Then subdue myself with pills

How can this stranger
Have such a familiar face
I left home over twenty years ago
Am I still in the same place ?

I'll learn to toil this soil by hand
I'll drink until I'm done
I'll run from those things I cannot face
I am not my father's only son

Cold

What is that in the underground?
Stirring way down below
Forgotten what to call it
For fear I'll let it show
I'll never let them know

I'll plug in the headphones
And just walk on by
Wear dark black sunglasses
To complete this disguise
This is all I know
To be a freak sideshow
But I won't let it show

No razor is sharp enough
To distract my pain
Maybe I'll use it
Just the same
For the only real thing
Is the world behind the eyes
And all those emotions
I've buried alive
So I got to keep up the show
And not let it show

If only the curtain would fall
I could cancel the show
What was once buried alive
Might begin to unfold
Then two would know
And half the load
But nobody knows

And this cold stony stare
That my sunglasses hide
Keeps others at arm's length
And the scars inside
For this disguise
Reminds me of somebody close
Who has forgotten how to feel
Or is too afraid to let it show
So I've got to cancel the show
Let the entire thing go
And everybody already knows

Air Born

There's someone I know
Who can teach you to fly
He's over 240 pounds
And six foot high
The ace of spades
Is in his hand
It's stacked against me
But I'll make a stand

Now's the time
I see it in his eyes
In one foul swoop
I begin to fly
One day I hope
To rise above
As for now
I receive his love

Don't give me this burden
I'll carry it for years
With scars on my wrist
And voices in my head
All these tears
I'll keep deep within
Like those other Schizos
From the Looney Bin
It's a temporary solution

Painting a permanent problem
For those surplus to requirements
Them beautiful unwanted

As for now
I'm learning to fly
I'd rather not
But he wants me to try

So jump on in
Come along
Together we'll sing
This melancholy song

So try
Take a dive
Come die with me

Medusa

I was only young back then
Full of life and folly
But that's a cruel mistake to make
According to those that ruled above me
For most of my life
I walked in fear
And four walls offer no protection
-when that giant I fear
-shadow appears

And its anger begins to stalk me

When you look into those eyes
Which reveals all its fury
Your spirit is slowly murdered
Your soul gradually buried
The Medusa stare
Turned my heart to stone
Bit by bit I retreated from life
I started to live alone

Now when I look into the mirror
I see that cold stony stare
Of the ugly Gorgon's head
That I always use to fear
Although it may take awhile
I will fight from year to year
To slay the Gorgon as Perseus did
And triumphantly hold high its head

The reflection of Medusa's eyes
Still chills me to the bone
At night when it's dark
And I'm home all alone
At least I know there's nobody around
Whose heart eye will turn to stone

Stranger

You're a perfect stranger
Who's shouts remain unheard
You're the brilliant poem
With neither rhyme, prose nor verse
A dunkard for a father
A schizo for a bro
The mother who shut the door
Then fed you to the cold
Friends gleam and shine
Relieve a hindered soul
Archetype of party animal
So loneliness remains alone
Stranger even more a stranger
Upon that foreign land
Where the finishing touches of a masterpiece
Of all my strangeness began
Coldness becomes a band-aid
Within the rocking chair years
We'll need more than denial
To reign in those fears
All those games and laughter
Couriered by a hearst

You think alcohol is needed
For an S.O.S. to be heard
You're a stranger's biography
Hidden in perfect code
You're the brilliant poem
Searching for it's prose

The Garden

There was once a garden
That use to thrive
Till everything inside
Began to die
Nobody knows exactly
When or why
Where blue skies had shined
On hopes and dreams
The thriving garden
Of all I could be
There's a well of tears
That now run dry
Else they've been driven
Deeper inside
All that's left
Inside walls of stone
Are weeds of hate
He calls his own

There was a garden
That use to thrive
Then bit by bit
Everything died
All who look
Will never know

That nothing's left
Except blood and bone
Like a slow cancer
He could no longer fight
Weeds consumed the garden
That had lived inside

That day the fear arrived

Somehow I must survive

PART TWO

Madness is a well for those who don't
realize they're thirsty

Cape Fear

This was my favorite film when I first started hearing voices. I admired the way Robert De Niro's character had to rebuild his life while he was in the can..."my mission during that time was to become more than human.."

I didn't realize it at the time but I'd become imprisoned by my own mind and just like Max Cady the only way out was to become more than human...but first I had to become less than.

Alive

It's been a twenty year roller coaster
One hell of a ride
The writings on the wall
I no longer need to hide
There's no red lights nor warning bells
Ringing in my head
You only have wisdom on the right shoulder
When you have the reaper on the left
I can see so clearly now
I no longer need to run
My executioners waiting in vain
I've already won
I'm on this path of self destruct
Today may be the day that I die
I feel this burning deep within
I've never felt so alive

Behind Bars

I live behind bars
But I've never been to prison
Met many kinds of people
But they've never crossed the chasm
Lived in houses
Never a home
Walked with others
But always alone
In my mind
There's a maze that weaves
Through hidden corridors
And forbidden streets
There's a wall I know
That's tall and high
No one gets to see
What's on the other side
Lived in houses
Never a home
Behind the bars
Sentence unknown

House of the Forgotten

I've got a new home for you
Your stay won't be for long
Although when you leave
It's influence will remain strong
There's a trolley full of lollies
Rooms to give you a break
People holding keys whispering
"It's your spirit we wish to take"
Every minute you'll count
Your torturer is time
You may have had a problem before
Now you surely want to die
This is the house of the forgotten
The downtrodden and ignored
Obey our rules insignificant one
Or be subject to our law

Merry Go Round

I've come to ride the merry go round
I've ridden it before
The last time nearly finished me
And left me wanting more
Some riders were familiar
Unable to get off
The ride had no monetary fee
So I reflected on the cost
Round and round we go
The ride we love and hate
Never knowing what got us here
Regretting the mistakes
Now I leave this merry go round
Pressing on one step at a time
Always knowing full well
I left a part of me behind

Give it a Name

Give it a name
So I know I am
Any term from the DSM
It's in your hands
Love and fear
Feel the same
All the nothingness
Subdues the pain
I've got the Schizo label
Been diagnosed with depression
Dabbled in self harm
And a checking obsession
Nothing seems to fit
The emptiness inside
A misfit of humankind
I can no longer hide
Give it a name
So whats lost can be found
Bring a spade or shovel
To find out what's underground
I hear the call weirdo
Maybe that's the truth
Not just another schizo or loser
That no one can get through

So I'll sit in that office
Look the genius in the eye
He'll prescribe me some pills
Then bid me 'goodbye'
What I feel
Isn't in a book
It's in the recess of my mind
But I'm too scared to look
So I'll keep on keeping on
Though it could all be in vain
When love and fear are indistinguishable
There's no longer any pain
And all the books in the world
Could never give that a name

Into the Fray

Never wanted to live so much
Such a high price to pay
I've loosened the grips of this jacket
As the seams begin to fray

The torments so beautiful
Volts run to my toes
The venom within their eyes
Fire inside their throats

I listen to the executioner's song
Knowing every word by heart
I return to the sanctuary of home
To tear myself apart

There is no empirical madness
No equation to love
I inject a perfect sadness
Then surrender to it's rush

So I choose neither hope nor madness
I choose neither fear nor fame
I choose the executioner's song
Or else I become its slave

Machine

It's just too powerful
I can't hold it back
This Machine has served me so well
Now I can't stop the attack
My eyes are blinded with vulnerability
I need to dock in this bay
Refuel and regroup
Machine is on his way
It's approaching with guns blazing
Now I'm under attack
It use to help me walk away
When I had knives stuck in my back
It's just too efficient
I need it to step aside
When I begin to approach the ledge
I retreat, turn back and hide
For this world is but an illusion
A maze within a maze
Machine seems so real to me
A dear friend that keeps me afraid

Tall

We have our arsenal at the ready
But the enemies pushing through
I use to go to the bayonet
When I started feeling blue
I hear my foes
Rapping on the walls
I've given too much
But he still wants it all
I'm a soldier of fortune
Opposing a formidable threat
Warring an invisible enemy
Inside my head
The combat is brutal
Bodies are piling up
Some friends of yesteryear
Have already given up
The weapons of our warfare
Are not guns and grenades
But a varying array of potions
Paints, pens and razor blades
It's a battle to the death
You've given it your all
On the morrow a new day dawns
For those who remain to again...
...stand tall

The Gem

Never forget the meaning of madness
Never relinquish those stolen years
Remember the gift of darkness
Genesis of your fear
All the pain you tried to forget
Shall be remembered with much more vigour
You'll start to connect the dots
Put the puzzle back together
There's monsters deep below
Hidden behind a mask
There's a blessing within a curse
If you're ever up to the task
Before you were made
Your destiny was foretold
Just like Perseus and Jason
Those brave heroes of old
You'll see Medusa's reflection
With your blind shield of faith
When bitterness, hardship and rejection
Have each had their taste
I had to wait patiently
For the calm after the storm
Peel back the layers of fear
From which I was born

There's light at the end of the tunnel
Right now it's so hard to see
So unlock the treasure within your darkness
The gem will set you free

Unite

I'm making giant steps
One sentence at a time
A new chapter has begun
With victory in my sight
A new day is dawning
The clouds have begun to lift
My thinkings correcting itself
As my consciousness starts to shift
Pain is not a currency
To be traded amongst friends
It's a life lesson to be learned
Not a position to defend
All the parts are starting to unite
From the four corners of my mind
After forty years of punishment
I'm forgiven of all my crimes
Now is the time to untangle
From this sinister web of deceit
Return to the river of life
Where I've begun to wet my feet
There's a new story to tell
Like those fables of old
Of lands far, far away

With streets paved of gold
Now I've begun to remember
All the dreams of my youth
A cloud has lifted as the parts unite
And I'm ready to see this through

PART THREE

Invisible Wars draw out Reluctant Heroes

Cinderella Man

One of my favorite scenes from Cinderella Man is when Jim Braddock goes begging for money to pay the power bill so he can get his kids back.

I'm sure most politicians would find this moving and yet there would be many eating out of dumpsters within their own electorate.

I myself find it hard to feel compassion for beggars. This from a guy who's been on welfare for an embarrassing long time. It's this kind of dissonance that creates a quandary inside of me. I feel torn between judgment and and my own self disgust.

It's a short journey between comfort and homelessness. Should l ever find myself in that situation then l hope those onlookers will see a fighter out of luck...rather than their own reflection.

Another Crusade

I'm defending this city
Steadfast and all alone
From all these slings and arrows
That cut me to the bone
I have guards on the towers
Keeping watch day and night
If I begin to feel too much
They'll set the defenses alight
My shield gives me protection
Though the battles already lost
Preserving the status quo
Regardless of the cost
Know that I don't hate you
Though I'll treat you with disdain
I've built this city
Brick by brick
From a legacy of pain
For one man's fears
Has become another's crusade
As the war inside continues
To push others away
My greatest fear
Is the thing I embrace the most
Even after all these years
I can't let it go

Making of Machine

Joined the chain
Faced the pain
Gave it my all
Again and again
Minute by minute
Seemed like hours on end
Do not fret
For in the end
Loaded gun
Is at my head
Pushing the limits
Towards the edge

These silent screams
Are all in vain
The epoch will tarry
Just the same

Cogs keep churning
From the team
I'm flying solo
Like a machine
Broke the lock

Cracked the code
Unveiled a secret
From days of old
Know what I need
To get ahead
Can't destroy
What's already dead
These silent screams
Are all in vain
The epoch will tarry
Just the same

Newman and Costner
Will stoke the desire
Monsters inside
Will sustain the fire
The harder it gets
The more I press
Know what it takes
To become the best
Lesson carved in
When I was little
As self preservation
Goes out the window

These silent screams
May all be in vain
The epoch will tarry
Just the same
But while my heart beats
On this earth
May it beat strong enough
To prove my self worth

Ed

When you look into that darkness
You see your own reflection
It reminds of the dragon
At the heart of your infection
Becoming a monstar
Is only a natural thing
So if I begin to cast a shadow
I'll stand firm-grit my teeth
Only the super inadequate
Feel like us
The socially inept
Incapable of trust

I hope I could never be
What you have become
But I think I understand
What made the darkness come

Where his life was gradually killed
A thousand different times
With all those demons
Dancing in his mind
Your lust for blood
Shall surely be relieved
As you stalk the prey

Unchain the beast
The monster slowly emerged
To temporarily subdue the pain
Of all that mud and rejection
Coursing through his veins

I hope I could never do
What you have done
But I think I understand
Why the evil won

Giant

There's a giant in my shadow
Lurking deep inside
Born from a kingdom of pain
The queen of the double bind
It roams endlessly day and night
When I choose to set it free
It tears apart its iron shackles
But I don't have the key
So tell me ' oh wise one'
"How to tame a giant?"
I have not nearly enough courage
And he's meaner than Goliath
I need to fight back today
Bring his reign to an end
I must slay him now or never
Before I start to run out of friends
So how do you slay a giant
Maybe one step at a time
I'm in shackles while he roams free
In the darkest region's on my mind
For some the darkness may fall
Sometimes the dragon will win
As for me and my Monster
I'll keep it locked within
Giant

The Mighty

The mighty need no reward
Their bravery is plain to see
They struggle and fight each day
It's dark when they reclaim the streets
No home in which to rest
No food to have their fill
Salvations found within a bottle
Redemptions contained in a pill
They're all part of a brotherhood
Like those noble knights of old
Memories haunt their kingdom
A story unable to be told
They have a breast plate of honour
Wear the helmet of clarity
Yield a sword known as resilience
And a shield called humility
If you ever see these noble knights
As they lay sleeping on the streets
And you know not what to do
Deciding to vote with your feet
Then go to places only they know
You'll realise they are you and me
Their honour was blinding your sight
Now they can reclaim the streets

Postponing the Reservation

A phoenix has risen
Renewed with anticipation
I've cancelled a desire
Postponing my reservation
I have hope within my belly
A heart flowing with desire
I've got seeds of burning ambition
To set this entire world on fire
A lion's stalking its prey
Ready to devour a beast
He will not let me rest nor slumber
Till his enemies have tasted defeat
When the tide of success has subsided
And I've shared the spoils of war
I'll search for other worlds to conquer
Remembering those who have gone before
It's the fallen who sustain the fire
At the center of my anticipation
I've cancelled a certain desire
Postponing the reservation

This World

I never did quite belong
Always afraid to feel
Quietly craving to reach out
I am not of this world
"We have no magic wands"
A nurse once said
As my voices taunted
And my wrists bleed
I have friends and family
I'm lucky to know
I can still make them all laugh
But inside it's cold
I have books and music
To make the hours go by
To find answers to the questions
In that journey of strife
Perhaps the greatest question
Is will I ever find that girl
Who'll subdue all my pain
And help me to feel
I want to reach out
So I know what's real
I look just like everyone else
I am not of this world

Dismantle

I must learn to dismantle him
Take apart machine
He use to keep me sane
When I heard my mother's screams
I need balance in my life
Machine won't let it show
He pushes people away
When I don't want them to go
I must repair its clouded eyes
Defrost his cold heart
As a daily conflict rages on
Tearing it's insides apart
There's scars on its armour
A darkness in his head
Memories of previous battles
Where the bravest soldiers won't be led
Machine sits idle for now
Ready to fight to the death
To protect and defend the status quo
Then ignore and delete the rest

Remember

When the dust has settled
And the battle is over
Will you remember me?
When the coffin is closed
And the service is over
Will you remember me?
As the seasons pass
And the years surrender
Will you remember?
Has this life been wasted
On the scars of yesteryear
Have I betrayed what's true
All I hold dear
Look the executioner
Square in the eye
Stand your ground
Before you die
For as the seasons pass
And the years surrender
I shall not surrender
I'll remember

PART FOUR

The Road to Certainty is Paved with many Graves

Edward Scissorhands

Ed's a pretty harmless guy except he has scissors for hands which (as you can imagine), makes physical contact a tad difficult. Although his face clean shaven he's not immune to the odd nick himself.

Ed was encouraged out of a secluded mansion by a nice lady wanting to help. Initially, everything was just dandy. Ed was giving killer haircuts to the local ladies and trimming hedges like Picasso.

But somewhere in between, he got lost. Or maybe what he was got lost in translation...at least in minds of others? But not everyone.

In one scene Ed rescues Kevin from being flattened by a van. Pretty noble...problem is everytime he reaches out he cuts without even trying.

As with others so it is with him.

Ed wants to belong but he can't trust others. However there are a few that can see past the scissors and don't mind the odd nick. It's not so much that Ed can't help cutting others, it's more that those who care don't feel the pain as much.

And remember this...Ed has to shave every day too.

The Breach

I've got to be honest with her
I must cancel the show
What was once buried alive
Has now begun to grow
I could to the cold thing for awhile
Watching you from afar
Knowing there's others around you
Trying to tear us apart
I'm right on the edge
At the precipice of change
What I feel for you is the only thing that's real
And it's never felt so strange
I need you more than water
A river could not quench this thirst
The dam holding back my emotions
Has breached its banks and begun to burst
I'm right on this precipice
Lost within a dream
Must be time to step over the ledge
And surrender this machine
I'm well over the threshold
Towards the point of no return
The outside is calm and collected
It's on the inside that I burn

Saturday Night Test

I see dark clouds coming
I'm preparing for a storm
The darkness and fear inside of me
Is slowly being reborn
So let me be that rock you depend on
Though the tempest is mighty and fierce
And I'll give you all that I am
Except the emptiness
I will never know
What we are nor who I am
So there's just one thing left
For us to comprehend
I see those dark clouds coming
The tempest is mighty and fierce
And what I feel is being battered and bruised
From all it's nothingness
Please dig me out of the rubble
When the chaos begins to subside
I'll be proud I made it this far
Then crawl back inside
Cause I don't know what I am to you
Is this just another Saturday night test?
So I'll give you everything I have to give
Until there's nothing left

Except the emptiness

Beautiful

They both knew the real score
That they belonged to losing teams
When his eyes conceded defeat
And her insides began to scream
He made scars in her honour
No other would ever see
All his guards had been over run
His city conquered and besieged
When his entire identity
Was consumed by a raging fire
His love remained unrequited
Returned just like a liar
She threw a going away party
For the friend that had disappeared
A bottle of pills was emptied
It's contents retained no fear
They loved each other so much
Desire was overcome
By feelings to scary to say
So they relinquished and began to run
When the Beautiful's had their fill
That's the only drug you'll desire
You'll become enamoured with a madness
Engulfed within it's fire

Home

I'm on a treacherous path
Trying to find a way home
Waiting for my spirit to return
To these mortal bones
This is a perilous journey
There may be danger around the bend
So I'll just wait patiently
For these feelings to end
There's a garden beyond the wall
Try and work your way through
The foliage is withered and dying
And I need to be true
You were the only shelter from the tempest
The only place that felt like home
You were the only harbour I could lay my anchor
The only place I ever belonged
I'm on this perilous journey
Weary and all alone
Waiting for my spirit to return
So I can find the way home

Song

I've continued to sing
A forgotten song
I remember those lyrics
When I'm all alone
Set free from a prison
For awhile
New images found
Stacked in a pile
You were the only one
To hack my mind
Draw the curtains
Pull back the blinds
The lost was found
The buried uncovered
My hurts sheltered
My fears smothered
Every dark soul
Needs a friend
Every solemn promise
Comes to an end
I know in time
I'll rise above
One day I hope
To be enough

Unknown

So afraid of this journey
Uncharted waters lay ahead
With unforgiving territory
The possibility of death
Not death of the physical
But finding an unknown land
Where the past can be put to rest
It's there I'll make my final stand
I'm ready to search for the grail
To succeed I must let go
Has it always been right before me?
Maybe I've always known
There's a hint of a mutiny
In our quest for that gift
I'm setting sail for an unknown territory
And I'm ready to abandon ship
It's a dangerous course we've set
Onto those yonder lands
Whatever lies beyond the horizon
I hope you'll understand
We're charting an unknown territory
With the possibility of death
The elusive grail is within our reach
I'm so afraid of what lies ahead

High Tide

I wandered one day
Through the forest of life
The canopy of the trees
Kept me tucked inside

Then I came to a river
At the end of it's road
Crossing would be treacherous
I'd be vulnerable and exposed

Bit by bit
I wet my feet
But before too long
I was in too deep

All that was bundled up
Gradually became untied
The flood was coming
It was nearly high tide

The scariest thing
Is letting someone inside
Sometimes you need to let go
In order to survive

I've been taken by this current
As I struggle and fight
Water fills my lungs
It's so good to be alive

ENCORE

Mad Max

I watched this movie as a kid so I may not have the best recollection of the plot. As best I remember though, Max is a 'lone wolf' whose only interest is surviving and getting petrol for his car.

He has no allegiance and no cause. It's only survival.

Then slowly he decides to help those who need it the most.

I don't know why certain people devote their entire lives to helping others. Yet it's these folk that seem to receive the most.

I couldn't imagine devoting my entire life to a single cause. But maybe just like Max I am...and I just haven't realized it yet?

The Insult

Most days
You can see me meandering
Placidly going about my business
Until l hear an insult
Then suddenly
Within a nano-second ...
...l can snap
And hear the deafening orders of pit-bulls
Readying to tear this insolence
Limb from limb
l feel a thirsty tomahawk
Ache for its blade to become soaked with fresh blood
As my other hand yields a knife
Eagerly awaiting its first scalp
Hard and erect in my palm
l yearn for my favourite blade
So l can at least etch a little validation
lnto my left wrist...
...Though in the end
l do none of these
But simply turn up my l-Pod
Smile politely
And continue on my way

Triumphant (OCD)

Obsessions a heavy yoke
The harder you try to throw it off, stronger its return
Like the girl you're too fearful to approach
Compulsions a wild beast
That never submits to brute strength
It stalks day and night with a fear of imperfection
Water may overflow
Drowning the floor with conditional love
Electricity could ignite
Turning this structure into a violent inferno
The fridge alone stands triumphant
During this suburban manslaughter
With its sealed doors and frozen innards

Sober

How could l ask her out ?
l'm a bumbling idiot
Who doesn't even feel comfortable in his own skin
How could l share it ?
l'm that song by ' Tool '
A worthless liar and imbecile
Who will only complicate you
l'm a salesman from the ' Fragil Wing '
With an unshakeable belief in the product
l'm the unkempt garden
Strangled by the weeds of timidity
l'm a religious zealot
Lost in his own theology
l am a Paranoid Schizophrenic
Who thinks his diagnosis will be enough
To see him through the empty years

Kingdom

Another Saturday afternoon
Listening to the ramblings of Mister Crazy
He jumps from subject to subject
Immune to his own frivolous voice
Absent from our surroundings,

Then l remembered how as a boy
l use to sit right up front at the Saturday matinees
Lost in a wonderland of heroes and villains
Reality would collapse around me
Crushed by its own weight
l thought to myself
"He's lost in the same kingdom"

Each sentence became beautifully mashed together
Bounded by a perfect chaos
With one hand he invites you in
While the other pushes you away
l felt the urge to tell him
"l know why you had to retreat from this world"
But l knew
If he had found out that l had broken the code
It would drive him deeper
In to the only place that ever made sense

Out of his League

1
lt's a Saturday afternoon
Over the next hour our group slowly pieces together
We laugh and joke
But our minds are preoccupied with other business
2
We nervously enter a room
To change and put the game face on
Our leader barks his orders, stoking the fire
Even the smell of liniment
Heightens the senses to the encroaching battle
Release me from this cage
So l can unload a blitzkrieg of rage
3
My warriors are in line
One of our opponents charges
So a teammate rams his shoulder into its side
[l secretly wish l can hear its ribs crack]
"Stick him" l cry "Fucken stick him"
Then another charges me
l lift him off his feet
Then return him crashing to the ground
"Go Chris" the crowd cheers
l return to my position

4
We cease
We shake hands
We eat
We drink
We laugh
Then head into town
Enemies within a brotherhood
Some as close as kin
5
l live for Saturday afternoons
I'm totally enamoured with this sanctioned thuggery, rugby
Nothing feels better than to return home after a hot shower
So my dented body can recover
Soaking up the pain like a satisfied masochist
lts my way of compensating for inadequacies
Purging an ugliness from within
6
Over the course of the following days
l replay [as we all do] the events of last week's game
The bad and the beautiful
Knowing if l played badly
l can redeem myself this coming Saturday
And if l played well
l get a fix as strong as any opiate

7
It's more than a game to me
It is me
As much as bone, muscle and sinew
Without it I am a rudderless ship
Lost in a vast ocean
Unlikely to find a way home
This is the brotherhood of blood
A game of redemption

Chasing Fire

I'm chasing fire
I've become mesmerized by its flame
Enamoured by its heat
If it becomes a raging inferno
Then I'll happily sacrifice myself

Am I a heretic to live with such danger?
It's not only devil's that love flames
There are many walking an edge
With Hades waiting below

We can tame fire
Forge blades within it that other empires will fear
We'll rule worlds
And capture unspeakable riches
It's fire that's manically moving my hand across this keyboard

Lest I lose it's magic

Fire can burn
But without it
My hand becomes static and lifeless

The Sharpest Sword

I live in a hightower
As I watch commoners below
Speak a strange tongue
Of which is incomprehensible
At least to me
I feign a persona of aloofness
Mistaken as conceit
Yet I crave the intricacies
Of their strange dialect

Each time I leave my tower
I fear being found out a fraud
My ignorance embarrases me
Yet it's my sharpest sword

Each time I venture into fields
I'm careful to tread well worn paths
I see youth drunk on their indifference
I was like that too once
Before conformity beat me down
And I was counted out
In the eleventh round

I long to drink the nectar of Aphrodite

For we were all sons of Zeus
Before we got lost in the truth
How would my ego survive
Without walls to contain it?

I'm a zealot to my self reliance
I preach independence
With the fervor of a TV evangelist
Who burns in the self contempt
Of his own duality

There are things we dare not wish for
Like breaking the enigma code
Of our own securities
Rolling the dice without influencing the outcome
And joining in on the celebration of uncertainty

I love shadows

For inside them
I can extract the essence of human nature
Then I understand myself better
I can draw out conclusions of the spirit
From double blind experiments

But shadows need light to ignite them
And I see a dragon hiding in hers
Subdued by our closest star
At least for now

However the clock is ticking...

...and the possibility of redemption
Grows gravely by the hour
As I return to the grave
In my high tower

The Obsessive Compulsive Disorder Prison

Thanks for reading my poetry book.

I've been involved with the psychiatric system and medication for over half my life. It has been a challenging journey.

Writing this poetry book has been a major therapeutic tool. My mental anguish has been transformed into gratitude. While this transition has been genuine it's still a position I find hard to accept.

The price has been high.

To be honest though my major contribution to the mental health community has been the creation of a memory system to beat my Obsessive Compulsive Disorder.

It doesn't help with all types of OCD.

But if you're a person that has compulsive checking, where you check things like the faucets, fridge door, front door, power outlets, coffee maker, and other things then I might be able to help you.

So if you fear that your house will be burgled or burnt down or become flooded then take a look at my website: strongerthanocd.com

Within this site you'll get FREE access to the memory tools and systems that help me to remember that everything is safely off, locked and closed.

Traditional therapy helps you overcome your compulsive checking by 'sitting' with doubt and uncertainty. You face your fears directly.

My system is not a therapy. It's based on memory techniques specifically designed help counter these symptoms .

I don't help you to live with doubt and uncertainty but to erase them all together.

No doubt => No uncertainty => No compulsive checking

You will still check but not as often and not as long. You can find out more at: strongerthanocd.com

Hey this is Chris. Should you need me for any reason then reach out to me at this email address or website.

Contact Details
Email: chris@chrismaoate.com
Website: strongerthanocd.com

'...that crown of thorns
was bound to tear
our brow and forehead
from ear to ear...'

unfinished poem

Each time I leave my tower
I fear being found out a fraud
My ignorance embrasses me
Yet it's my sharpest sword

The possibility of redemption
Grows gravely by the hour
As I return to the grave
In my high tower